Collins

Enhanced Engaging English 2

Workbook

Name: ______________________

Grade: ________ Section: ________

Somali Mitra

HarperCollins*Publishers*

Publishing operations in 17 countries and 120+ imprints globally

William Collins' dream of knowledge for all began with the publication of his first book in 1819. A self-educated mill worker, he not only enriched millions of lives, but also founded a flourishing publishing house. Today, staying true to this spirit, Collins books are packed with inspiration, innovation and practical expertise. They place you at the centre of a world of possibility and give you exactly what you need to explore it.

Published by Collins Learning
An imprint of HarperCollins*Publishers* India
Building No. 10, Tower A, 4th Floor, DLF Cyber City, Gurugram, Haryana 122002, India

Revised edition: 2025
Reprint: 10 9 8 7 6 5 4 3 2 1
ISBN: 978-93-6569-928-9
Printed and bound in India by MicroPrints India, New Delhi

Browse the complete Collins catalogue at www.collins.in.
For any queries/feedback, please write to us at SCHOOLSUPPORT@harpercollins.co.in.

Preface

Enhanced Engaging English aims to instill an appreciation for literature in today's learners, while equipping them with the tools to develop native fluency and communicative competence in using the English language. The eight-level series comprises Coursebooks, Workbooks, and digital resources for teachers for all levels.

The revised edition has been aligned closely with the guidelines of the National Curriculum Framework, 2023 through its focus on twenty-first century skills, Sustainable Development Goals (SDGs), cross-curricular learning, 'Happiness' content and art-integrated learning. Coursebooks and Workbooks 1 and 2 integrate the essence of NIPUN (National Initiative for Proficiency in Reading with Understanding and Numeracy). They aim to motivate students to read independently, improve their vocabulary, develop their critical thinking and creative skills and enhance their ability to express themselves verbally and in writing.

The lessons are built around carefully selected literary pieces with distinct cross-curricular themes, and presented with glossary, explanation of literary terms and interesting trivia. The end-of-chapter exercises address the needs of formal language learning.

The **Workbooks** are designed to complement the Coursebooks, by providing additional skills practice, review and assessments. They comprise the following sections:

Comprehension includes factual, inferential and evaluative questions based on short reading passages.

Way with Words includes exercises on the vocabulary topics encountered in the Coursebook as well as extension activities derived from it. It also incorporates activities on literary devices and figures of speech, spelling drills and exercises on dictionary usage.

Grammar in Use starts with a short explanation of important grammar concepts covered in the Coursebook, followed by plenty of practice for reinforcement.

Listening and Speaking builds students' oral and aural communication skills. It includes tasks such as phonics drills, conversation practice, role plays and debates to develop spoken English skills. Listening comprehension exercises teach students to listen for both general and specific details. In poetry chapters, there are activities on stress, rhyme and metre.

Pen it Down: The activities in this section include guided and free writing tasks derived from the reading text, which build on the functional and creative writing skills of the learner.

Each Workbook also contains two **Tests**. One of these is based on the principle of SAFAL (Structured Assessment For Analyzing Learning), a competency-based assessment introduced by CBSE. They assess the competencies of critical thinking as well as inquiry-based and analysis-based learning. The other test is modelled on class assessments.

The series encourages competency-based education which allows concept acquisition at the learner's own pace, based on individual ability. We hope that it will foster a love for literature and reading in young learners.

Detailed Contents

Unit	Themes	Way with Words	Grammar in Use	Listening and Speaking	Pen it Down
1. The Lost Sock	Family	• Contextual usage • Compound words	• Common and special names • Doing words	• Listening and writing true/false • Talking on a given topic	• Rearranging pictures and writing the story
2. The Farmer, His Son and the Donkey	Fable	• Naming words: singular and plural	• Punctuation: capital letters and full stop • Using *is/am/are*	• Listening and choosing correct answers • Role-play: using polite words	• Writing lines on a given topic
3. The Elephant	Animals	• Opposite words • Animal sounds	• Using *do/does* for questions	• Listening and writing words • Looking at pictures and identifying feelings	• Writing a poem
4. A Holiday Letter	Travel	• Word groups • Naming words: gender	• Types of sentences: statement and question • Punctuation: comma, question mark and exclamation mark	• Listening to and saying words with silent vowel sounds • Role-play: conversation on a given topic	• Completing a story and drawing and colouring a picture related to it
5. Anansi and the Feast of Yams	Food	• Opposite words • Words beginning with *sp-* and *st-*	• Describing words • Tenses: simple present, simple past	• Listening to instructions and drawing and colouring a picture	• Writing lines about the characters in a story
6. The Boy and the Kite	Unexpected Friendships	• Nesting words • Professions	• Subject-verb agreement	• Listening to and answering *do/does* questions	• Colouring a picture and writing sentences
7. Sea Creatures	Under the Sea	• One syllable words • Similar sounding words	• Countable and uncountable naming words • Doing words with *-ing*	• Reciting a poem	• Looking at a picture and answering questions
Test-1					
8. A Visit to the Library	Books and Reading	• Words related to books	• Posessive pronouns • Regular and irregular verbs	• Speaking on a given topic	• Writing a paragraph on a given topic

Unit	Themes	Way with Words	Grammar in Use	Listening and Speaking	Pen it Down
9. Hiding	Actions	• Homophones • Rhyming words	• Apostrophe for possession • Apostrophe for contractions • Using *has/have*	• Pair work: conversation on a given topic	• Writing sentences on a given topic
10. The Hen and the Apple Tree	Moral Tales	• Words beginning with *cr-* • Words ending in *-st*	• Prepositions • Adverbs	• Listening to and solving riddles	• Completing an informal letter
11. There was Once a Puffin	Feathered Friends	• Rhyming words	• Doing words • Question words	• Group discussion on planning a programme	• Writing a paragraph on a given topic
12. The Big Fight	The World Around Us	• Words related to cats and dogs • Word meanings	• Comparative adjectives • Using *myself, yourself, himself, herself*	• Speaking on a given topic	• Writing sentences
13. Too Much Noise	Neighbourhood and Community	• Two syllable words	• Articles: *a, an* and *the* • Simple future tense	• Giving suggestions • Story building using story ball	• Writing a dialogue on a given topic
14. My Dad, He Wears Glasses	Everyday Objects	• Opposite words	• Conjunctions: *and, or, but*	• Listening to instructions and colouring • Talking about losing something and finding it	• Writing a short poem using rhyming words
15. The Bremen Town Musicians	Music	• Names of professions • Anagrams	• Forming negative sentences • Using *much/many*	• Listening to descriptions and identifying animals • Enacting a scene from a play	• Writing a story using clues
Test-2					

Contents

1 The Lost Sock

Comprehension

Read the story carefully and answer the questions.

Miss Sunflower was crying.

'A thief just stole my pumpkin pie! Now what will I have for dinner?' she sobbed.

'Don't cry, Miss Sunflower. We will find your pumpkin pie,' said Officer Zig.

'We will catch that crook!' said Officer Zag.

'Look! There he goes!' said the policemen.

'I'm too fast and you're too slow. You will never catch the pumpkin pie thief!' cried the crook.

They chased him up the hill, but the crook was too quick.

They chased him down the riverbank, but the crook rolled away.

They chased him under the bridge, but the crook swam away. They chased him around the tree, but they could not catch the crook.

Officer Zig and Officer Zag did not give up. They ran and ran.

SPLAT! They chased him right into a wall!

'Hurray! We caught the crook!' said the brave men.

Officer Zig and Officer Zag gave the pumpkin pie back to Miss Sunflower.

'Thank you very much,' said Miss Sunflower.

Tick (✓) the correct options.

1. Miss Sunflower was crying because

   a. she was hungry. ☐ b. a thief stole her pumpkin pie. ☐

2. The names of the policemen were

   a. Zig and Zag. ☐ b Tom and Jerry. ☐

3. They chased the pumpkin thief

a. up the tower. ☐ b. down the riverbank. ☐

4. They caught the pumpkin thief when he

a. ran into a pond. ☐ b. ran into a wall. ☐

5. Miss Sunflower wanted to have the pumpkin pie for

a. dinner. ☐ b. tea. ☐

Way with Words

Contextual Usage

A. Fill in the blanks with the correct words from the box.

officer	pumpkins	crook	bridge	chased	policemen

1. The __________ snatched the old lady's bag.
2. The dog __________ the cat up the tree.
3. The two __________ caught the thief quickly.
4. There is a __________ over the river.
5. The __________ looked smart in his uniform.
6. The farmer grew huge __________ in his field.

Compound Words

B. Match the words in Column A with those in Column B to form compound words. Then write the compound words under the pictures.

Column A	Column B
1. mail	a. cake
2. farm	b. pot
3. pan	c. house
4. jelly	d. ground
5. tea	e. box
6. play	f. fish

					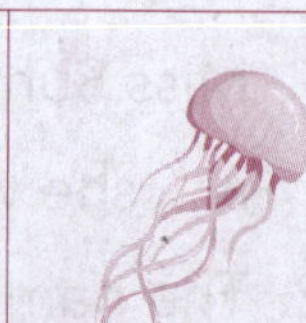
1.__________	2.__________	3.__________	4.__________	5.__________	6.__________

Grammar in Use

Common and Special Names

We use **common names** to refer to people, places, animals, and things in general.

Examples: officer, girl

We use **special names** to identify any one person, place, animal or thing.

Examples: Officer Zig, Miss Sunflower

A. Read the passage. Circle the common names and underline the proper names in it. Then, make sentences with any three of the common names.

Today is the first day of June. Mrs Gomes is teaching her class. She is writing on the blackboard with a chalk and is using a duster to clean the board. Mrs Gomes asks Raina a question. Raina does not know the answer. Mrs Gomes asks Nikhil the same question. All the children have their books open in front of them and they are all holding pencils. There are charts on the wall showing spaceships and an imaginary planet called Argos. Lily is sitting quietly at her desk, next to her friend, Soumya.

1. ____________________

2. ____________________

3. ____________________

B. Look at the pictures. Find the names of these animals in the word grid.

d	o	g	c	f
l	d	o	o	i
a	f	l	m	s
c	h	d	l	h
a	p	f	t	m
t	a	b	u	c
o	r	s	r	h
a	r	p	t	a
r	o	u	l	r
d	t	j	e	t

Doing Words

You know that a word that shows action is called a **verb** or a **doing word**.

Examples: The thief **runs** with the pie.

The officers **chase** the thief.

The words **runs** and **chase** are doing words because they show action.

C. Underline the doing words in these sentences.

1. The cows roam in the field.
2. Tom chases Jerry all around the house.
3. The sun rises in the east every day.
4. Monkeys eat bananas.
5. I read a story to my sister every night.
6. Mother scolds me when I am naughty.

Listening and Speaking

A. Listen to a passage and write if the sentences are true (T) or false (F).

1. It is not wonderful to have pets. ☐
2. We should look after our pets. ☐
3. Dogs do not need daily exercise. ☐
4. We should not take our pets to the vet. ☐
5. Pets can be our best friends. ☐

B. Imagine that you live in a magical land where all the food we eat can talk to us. What would you say to the following food items?

Example: cheese: I want to put you on my bread every day.

1. milk
2. strawberry
3. ice cream
4. toast
5. omelette
6. muffins

Pen it Down

Look at the pictures and rearrange the sentences to make a story. Write the sentences together as a paragraph.

- She gives the kitten warm milk to drink and takes care of it.
- The little kitten becomes Sheena's best friend and they play together.
- She brings the kitten home.
- Sheena goes to play with her friends.
- She sees a little kitten lying in the cold.

Fable

2 The Farmer, His Son and the Donkey

Comprehension

Read the story carefully.

Once, a hungry wolf was eating too greedily, and a big bone got stuck in his throat. It did not move up or down. He could not eat a thing. The wolf was very sad.

He decided to ask the crane for help. He was sure that she, with her long neck and bill, would be able to pull it out.

'I will give you a reward,' said the wolf, 'if you pull the bone out for me.'

The crane was scared to put her head in the wolf's mouth. But she was greedy too and wanted the reward. So, she did what the wolf asked her to do.

The crane pulled out the bone and the wolf was happy. He started to walk away.

'But what about my reward?' shouted the crane.

'You already have it. I did not bite your head, did I?' said the wolf, and left.

A. Answer in one word.

1. What had got stuck in the wolf's throat? ____________
2. What kind of neck did the crane have? ____________
3. What did the wolf promise the crane? ____________
4. What feeling did the crane have about putting her head in the wolf's mouth? ____________
5. What word can you use to describe the crane? ____________

B. Read the line and answer the questions.

'But what about my reward?'

a. Who said these words and to whom?

____

b. Why was the speaker going to be rewarded?

c. What reward did she get finally?

Way with Words

Naming Words: Singular and Plural

A. Rearrange the jumbled words that are in the plural forms. Then write their singular forms. One is done for you.

Jumbled Words	Plural	Singular
1. *miec*	*mice*	*mouse*
2. leasev		
3. potoesta		
4. knisve		
5. teesr		
6. bsuse		

B. Rewrite the sentences with the plural forms of the underlined words. You may have to make other necessary changes.

1. The woman and her child are going to the market.

2. I do not like to eat a sandwich for breakfast.

3. They have a party every weekend in winter.

4. The car is parked in the garage.

5. My foot is aching.

6. I have kept a loaf of bread on the table.

7. The fox is hiding behind the bush.

8. I can see a fish in the aquarium.

Grammar in Use

Punctuation: Capital Letters and Full Stop

Capital letters are used at the beginning of a sentence. **Full stops (.)** are used to end a sentence.

Example: **H**e could not eat a thing**.**

A. Rewrite the passage correctly. Add capital letters and full stops wherever required.

nehal and jeeya went to water kingdom today they had a great time their friends ashish and rohan, also went with them it was the month of april but it was not very hot nehal said to ashish, 'Do you want to ride the moonraker?' ashish was very excited and said, 'Hurrah, let's ride it!' after they finished all the rides, the four of them ate sandwiches, cookies, apples and fruits they had a wonderful day

Using Is, Am and Are

You have learnt that we use *is* when we talk about one subject and *are* when we talk about more than one subject. We use *am* with I.

Examples: The wolf **is** very sad.

The animals **are** scared of the wolf.

I **am** so hungry.

B. Rewrite the sentences by correcting the underlined words.

1. I is going to the library.

____

2. The cat are under the chair.

____

3. Ms Bharadwaj am my Hindi teacher.

____

4. There is many kittens in the basket.

____

5. The fruits is on the table.

____

6. The children am making a lot of noise.

____

Listening and Speaking

A. Listen to the passage and choose the correct options.

1. The two boys were at the ____________.

a. bus stop b. park

2. One of the boys was ____________.

a. afraid b. asleep

3. The other boy gave the dog ____________.

a. meat b. biscuits

4. The dog's name was ____________.

a. Hector b. Bruno

5. The owner thanked the brave boy and gave him ____________.

a. chocolates b. strawberries

B. Work in pairs and role play a conversation between a boy and an old lady who are travelling on the same bus together. Remember to speak politely. You can start the conversation like this:

Boy: Granny, would you like this seat?

Old Lady: Oh yes, thank you. I am rather tired.

Boy: You are most welcome, Granny.

Pen it Down

Write a few lines about an incident when you did something wrong and learnt a lesson from it.

You may include these points:

- I was not telling the truth and I got caught.
- I did not know that I would be punished.
- I realized my mistake.
- I learnt my lesson.

3

The Elephant

Way with Words

Opposite Words

A. Rewrite the sentences with the opposites of the underlined words.

1. You need not laugh, it is not that funny.
2. The boy always comes early to school.
3. This bag is too heavy for me.
4. That loaf of bread is stale.
5. Meera always leaves her room very tidy.
6. This car is quite slow.
7. Your uniform is dirty.
8. Your room is smaller than mine.
9. She likes to drink cold coffee.
10. These questions are very easy.

Animal Sounds

B. Look at the names of some animals. Then write the name of each animal's baby and the sound the animal makes. One is done for you.

1. lion → *cub* / *roar*

2. cat

3. owl

4. horse

5. cow

Grammar in Use

Using Do/Does for Questions

When we ask someone directly about things in the present, we use *do* at the beginning of the question.

Examples: Do you like animals? **Do** the elephants live in the jungle?

When we ask a question about someone else, we use *does* at the beginning of the question.

Examples: Does Sumeet have a pet? **Does** the elephant have big ears?

Do/Does questions usually have *yes/no* answers.

Read the sentences and form questions using do or does.

Example: I want to go home.

<u>*Do you want to go home?*</u>

1. Yes, mother needs help in the kitchen.

____

2. Yes, the team needs special coaching.

____

3. No, I do not want a burger.

____

4. No, I do not need to go by car.

____

5. Yes, my brother knows how to drive.

____

6. Yes, I play the guitar.

____

Listening and Speaking

A. Listen to the words and write them down.

____

____

____

____

____

B. Look at these faces. Each face expresses a feeling. Work in pairs. Identify the feeling and tell your partner what it is.

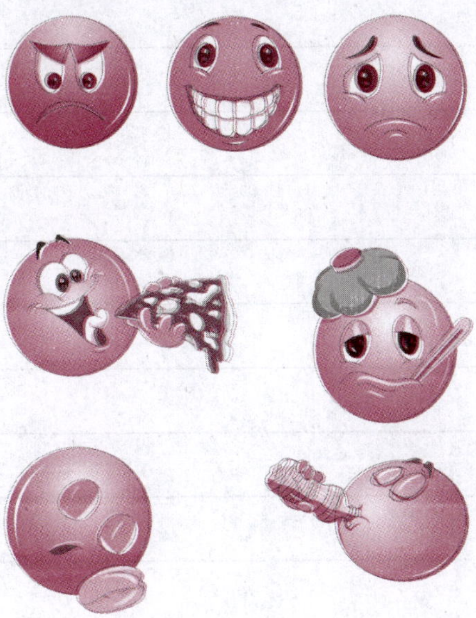

Pen it Down

Read the given rhyming words. Write a simple four-line poem using these word pairs.

- cake, bake
- talk, walk
- well, fell
- cook, look
- smile, while
- try, fly

4

Travel

A Holiday Letter

Comprehension

Read the passage carefully and answer the questions.

During my summer holidays, we went to the Jim Corbett National Park. It is named after the famous author and hunter, Jim Corbett. I was very excited and packed my bag three days before we were to leave. After flying to Delhi, we went by car to the park. The next morning, we went on a safari in an open jeep. It was quite early, and still dark, when we reached the park gates. I sat close to my mother looking at the sights and listening carefully for animal sounds. I had to be very quiet as animals do not like noise. As we were driving across grassy fields and dry riverbeds, I saw herds of deer and groups of monkeys. We could hear the calls of the barking deer, and we even saw a large stag.

Although all of us were waiting to spot a tiger, none could be seen. However, we did see a black bear climbing up a rocky cliff with a baby bear clinging to its back. My father took lots of pictures and I also looked through his binoculars. All day we roamed the park, watching different types of birds, deer, and elephant herds. It was such an exciting trip! I learnt how important it is for us to respect all creatures.

A. Match the sentence halves to complete them.

A	B
1. We went on a holiday	to Delhi.
2. We took a flight	lots of pictures.
3. We went to the park	his binoculars.
4. My father took	to Jim Corbett National Park.
5. I looked through	in an open jeep.

B. Answer the questions in brief.

1. Why was it dark when the people reached the park gates?

____

____

2. Why had the speaker been asked to be quiet?

____

____

3. Which animal did they hear calling?

____

____

4. Who was climbing up the rocky cliff?

____

____

Way with Words

Word Groups

A. Look at the words in the cloud and put them into the correct columns.

shark leopard cherry bookshelf
refrigerator armchair lorry teddy bear
pencil table hippopotamus mango
airplane diary watermelon eraser
doll oven bus puzzle ruler television
gorilla cycle

animals	furniture	appliances	toys	stationery	transport

Naming Words: Gender

The **gender** of a naming word tells us if it is masculine or feminine.
Examples: I sat close to my **mother** looking at the sights.
My **father** took lots of pictures.

B. Rewrite the sentences after changing the gender of the words in italics. You may have to make other necessary changes.

1. The *prince* was practising with his sword.

2. The farmer has two *bulls* and three *drakes.*

3. Do you have any *brothers*?

4. My *niece* is arriving from England tomorrow.

5. The *lady* and her *maidservant* came in the carriage.

6. These gardens are full of *peacocks.*

7. The *hero* of the film is a tall *man.*

8. The *king* is visiting the neighbouring kingdom.

Grammar in Use

Types of Sentences

You know that there are different types of sentences.

A **statement** gives some information and ends with a full stop.

Example: The next morning, we went on a safari.

A **question** asks for some information and ends with a question mark.

Example: Did the boy look through the binoculars?

A. Read the following sentences and identify their types.

1. Ravi left for his village today. ____________
2. Will he return next week? ____________
3. Don't you like bananas? ____________
4. I had a fruit shake for breakfast. ____________
5. Ribhu and Sushma had a fight. ____________
6. Why do you always fight with each other? ____________

Punctuation: Comma, Question Mark and Exclamation Mark

A **comma (,)** is used to separate things on a list.

Example: We saw different types of birds**,** deer**,** and elephant herds.

Question marks (?) are used at the end of a question.

Example: Did you see the black bear**?**

Exclamation marks (!) are used at the end of sentences which show a strong feeling.

Example: It was such an exciting trip**!**

B. Punctuate the sentences using capital letters, question mark, exclamation mark and full stop wherever necessary.

1. ruhi and shyamal are arriving in delhi on Thursday

____

____

2. do you understand what i am asking

____

____

3. may and june are the summer months all across india

4. mr gomes is working for cadburys

5. can you please ask my mother to call me

6. robinson crusoe is the name of my favourite book

7. have you watched the sound of music

8. sheetal is going to study with siya

9. I hate mondays

10. hurrah the holidays start tomorrow

Listening and Speaking

A. Listen to and repeat the words with silent vowel sounds.

B. Imagine that you are in a shop buying food items. Work in pairs and role-play a conversation. Your partner is the shopkeeper and you are asking for his help as you shop.

You may begin like this:

Student 1: May I know the price of this packet of chips?

Student 2: Ten rupees.

Student 1: Is there anything cheaper?

Pen it Down

Read the beginning of a story.

The day began with dark clouds in the sky. Soon it started raining. Mother asked Tejas not to go to school. He sat by the window looking out. He saw a poor kitten on the street shivering in the rain. Tejas called his mother. When she came, he showed her the wet kitten.

Mother said…

What do you think happens next? Complete the story in your own words.

Draw and colour a picture to show how the story ends.

5 Anansi and the Feast of Yams

Comprehension

Read the story carefully.

Once upon a time, there lived a spider named Anansi. Anansi loved to taste the food that people in the village made at home for their families.

One day, he stopped by Rabbit's house. Rabbit was his good friend.

'There are greens in your pot,' cried Anansi excitedly. Anansi loved greens.

'They are not quite done,' said Rabbit. 'But they will be soon. Stay and eat with me.'

'I have some things to do, Rabbit,' Anansi said quickly. If he waited at Rabbit's house, he was sure Rabbit would give him work to do. 'I know,' said Anansi. 'I'll spin a web. I'll tie one end around my leg and one end to your pot. When the greens are done, tug on the web, and I'll come running!'

Rabbit thought that was a great idea. And so, it was done.

'I smell sweet potatoes,' Anansi sniffed happily as he walked along. 'Sweet potatoes and honey!'

'Anansi,' called his friend, Bear. 'My pot is full of sweet potatoes and honey! Come share my food with me.'

'Sure!' said Anansi. Once again, Anansi suggested he spin a web, with one end tied around his leg, and one end tied to the sweet potato pot.

His friend, Bear, thought that was a great idea. And so, it was done.

By the time Anansi arrived at the river, he had one web tied to each of his eight legs with the other end tied to different pots of food.

'This was a wonderful idea,' Anansi told himself. 'I wonder whose pot will be ready first?'

Just then, Anansi felt a tug at his leg. 'Ah,' said Anansi. 'That is the web string tied to Rabbit's greens.' He felt another. And another. Anansi was pulled three ways at once.

'Oh dear,' said Anansi, as he felt the fourth pull.

Just then, he felt the fifth web string tug. And the sixth. And the seventh. And the eighth. Anansi was pulled this way and that way. His legs were pulled thinner and thinner. Anansi rolled himself into the river to wash away all the webs.

'Maybe that was not such a good idea after all,' said Anansi.

To this day, Anansi has eight very thin legs. And he never got any food that day at all!

Answer the questions in brief.

1. What was Rabbit cooking?

   ____

2. Why was Anansi in a hurry to leave Rabbit's house?

   ____

3. What was in Bear's pot?

   ____

4. What did Anansi suggest to his friends?

   ____

5. What did Anansi feel once he reached the river?

   ____

6. Why did he roll himself into the river?

   ____

Way with Words

Opposite Words

A. Fill in the blanks with the opposites of the words given in the brackets.

1. My brother likes to eat ______________ fruits. (stale)
2. I can carry the ______________ suitcase. (heavy)
3. My father likes to sleep on a ______________ mattress. (hard)
4. Rahul always keeps his ______________ room tidy. (large)
5. The horse jumped over the ______________ fence. (low)
6. The road is ______________ and curved at this point. (wide)
7. The ______________ fox fooled the crocodile. (foolish)
8. The ______________ farmer was rewarded by the king. (dishonest)
9. The ______________ noise woke up the baby. (soft)
10. It was a ______________ and sunny day. (cold)

Words With sp- And st-

B. Look at the pictures and write the correct words beginning with sp- or st-.

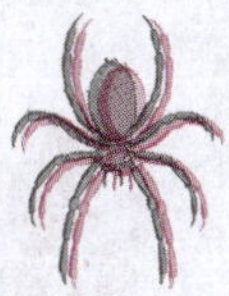 1. ____________	 2. ____________	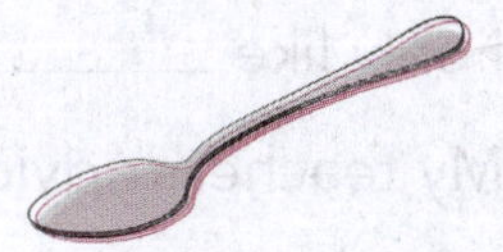 3. ____________
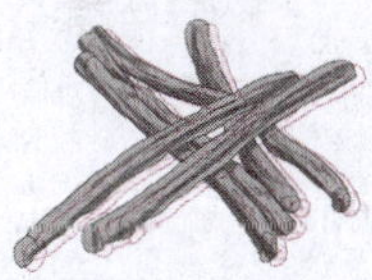 4. ____________	 5. ____________	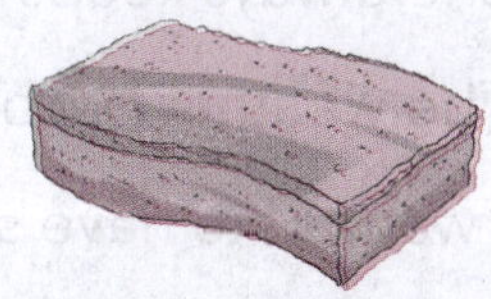 6. ____________

Grammar in Use

Describing Words

You have learnt that **describing words** or **adjectives** give more details about naming words.

Examples: Rabbit was his **good** friend. Rabbit thought that was a **great** idea.

A. Choose five words from the box that describe you.

cheerful	friendly	quiet	tall	shy	active	graceful	healthy
smart	pretty	fit	forgetful	intelligent	quick	loud	short

__________ __________ __________ __________ __________

B. Fill in the blanks with the correct describing words.

tight long sticky muddy easy

1. I hope the test will be __________.
2. Mysha's shoes are so __________ that her feet are hurting.
3. That dog's paws are __________ from running around in the garden.
4. Raani's fingers were __________ after having candy floss.
5. Marina has ____________ silky hair.

C. Complete the sentences using the describing words given in the box.

freezing	prickly	loud	heavy
empty	sweet	helpful	clean

1. I only like ____________ candies, not the sour ones.
2. My teacher's advice is ____________.
3. Rohit could not lift the ____________ box.
4. The cactus in the desert is ____________.
5. She always keeps her room very tidy and ____________.
6. The weather becomes ____________ in winter.
7. I wanted to have some chocolates, but the box was completely ____________.
8. We were all dancing to the ____________ music.

PRESENT AND PAST TENSES

You know that tenses tell us when an action happened.

We use the **present tense** to talk about an action happening now.

Example: 'I **smell** sweet potatoes,' Anansi sniffed happily as he walked along.

We use the **past tense** to talk about an action that has happened before.

Example: Once upon a time, there **lived** a spider named Anansi.

D. Complete the table with the correct forms of the verbs. One is done for you.

Present	Present with *-ing*	Past
1. *take*	*taking*	*took*
2.	baking	
3.		wrote
4. try		
5.		cooked
6.	smiling	
7. think		
8.		brought

Listening and Speaking

Listen to the instructions carefully and draw a diagram on food.

Healthy Food	Junk Food

Pen it Down

Complete the lines based on your understanding of Anansi and his friends.

'Come and share my food with me.'

This tells us that Bear was...

____

____

'I would love to but I have things to do.'

This tells us that Anansi was...

____

____

'Stay and eat with me.'

This tells us that Rabbit was...

____

____

6

The Boy and the Kite

Comprehension

Read the story carefully and answer the following questions.

Once upon a time, a beautiful princess was playing with her golden ball in the garden. She threw the ball high but alas! The ball fell into a deep well. The princess cried and cried because she loved her ball.

'Don't cry, I will get your ball for you,' she heard a voice say. She looked up and saw a little green frog. 'But if I get your ball, you will have to let me sleep and eat with you,' said the frog.

The princess agreed. The frog jumped into the well and came out with her golden ball. Then he hopped onto her arm and went with her to the palace. The princess was not happy to sleep beside him on her cozy bed and share her delicious food with him. But she had promised to do so.

One day, she was very angry with the frog and threw him off her bed. The frog fell on the floor and turned into a handsome prince. A wicked witch had cursed the prince and turned him into a frog. The princess married the prince and they lived happily ever after.

Arrange the sentences according to the order of events in the story.

- ☐ One day, she was angry with the frog and threw him off the bed.
- ☐ The princess was playing with her golden ball which fell into a well.
- ☐ She married the prince and they lived happily ever after.
- ☐ The princess was not happy to have the frog with her, but she had to keep her promise.
- ☐ A witch had cursed the prince and turned him into a frog.
- ☐ The frog promised to bring her the ball if she would let him live with her.
- ☐ She heard a frog say that he would get her ball.
- ☐ After she got her ball back, the frog ate and slept with her.
- ☐ The frog turned into a prince.

Way with Words

Nesting Words

A. Find the smaller words hidden in these words.

1. scare ____________________
2. horse ____________________
3. earth ____________________
4. looped ____________________
5. sales ____________________
6. lady ____________________
7. croak ____________________
8. brake ____________________

Professions

B. Match these people with the places where they work.

A	B
1. dentist	a. ship
2. pilot	b. bakery
3. farmer	c. workshop
4. postman	d. dental chamber
5. baker	e. kitchen
6. chef	f. farm
7. mechanic	g. aircraft
8. captain	h. post office
9. teacher	i. laboratory
10. scientist	j. school

Grammar in Use

Subject-Verb Agreement

You have learnt that a verb must always agree with its subject in number.
Singular verbs are used with singular subjects.
Example: The princess **marries** the prince.
Plural verbs are used with plural subjects.
Example: All frogs **are** not princes.

A. Complete the sentences with the correct verbs from the brackets.

1. Riya ________________ (love/loves) her pet dog.
2. The dog ________________ (plays/play) in her yard all day long.
3. He ________________ (run/runs) after the red ball and ________________ (chase/chases) the butterflies.
4. The neighbours ________________ (laugh/laughs) at him.
5. Cats ________________ (get/gets) scared of him and run away from the yard.
6. Riya ________________ (think/thinks) that she has the world's funniest dog.

B. Complete the sentences with was or were.

1. Shilpa ________ not at school yesterday.
2. Many people ________ there on my birthday.
3. They ________ really excited about the trip.
4. This game ________ so much fun!
5. The questions in the maths test ________ very tricky.

Listening and Speaking

Questions can be formed using the words *do* or *does*.

Examples: **Do** you like chocolate?
Does the princess like the frog at first?

Work in pairs and take turns to ask the following questions with *do/does* about dogs. Answer in your own words to your partner.

1. Do you like dogs?
2. Does a dog like to be taken out for walks?
3. Do dogs like to play?
4. Does a dog live in a kennel?
5. Do dogs purr?
6. Does a dog need to be fed regularly?

Pen it Down

Colour the picture of the fairy and describe her in a few sentences. Use the words from the help box.

fairy princess	magical powers	magic wand	fairy land

7

Sea Creatures

Way with Words

One Syllable Words

A single syllable word has one uninterrupted vowel sound.
Examples: work silk bird talk

A. Identify and write the single syllable words from the box in the blanks.

cotton	wool	tiger	baby	tree	mango	egg
teddy	bug	snake	mother	sock	dress	yellow

1. ____________
2. ____________
3. ____________
4. ____________
5. ____________
6. ____________
7. ____________

Similar Sounding Words

B. Circle the correct word to complete the sentences.

1. Last night, we (ate/eight) pizza for dinner.
2. Mt. Everest is the highest mountain (peek/peak) in the world.
3. Alice jumped into the rabbit (whole/hole).
4. I often (write/right) poetry.
5. We will (be/bee) watching the football match tonight.

6. Can you (sea/see) what is written on the blackboard?
7. The brave (knight/night) fought the dragon.
8. The old man asked his (son/sun) to take the goat to the market.
9. Does this shop (cell/sell) chocolates?
10. (I/Eye) had met my friend yesterday.

Grammar in Use

Countable and Uncountable Naming Words

Countable naming words are those that we can count by using numbers.

Example: I see <u>three</u> **frogs** croaking.

Uncountable naming words are those that cannot be measured by using numbers.

Example: I put **salt** in my tea.

A. Match the countable nouns with their uncountable categories.

Countable Nouns	Uncountable Categories
1. books	a. baking
2. experiments	b. furniture
3. cakes	c. wildlife
4. animals	d. knowledge
5. chairs	e. science
6. paintings	f. sports
7. balls	g. art

Doing Words with -ing

We use the **present continuous tense** for actions that are going on at the present time.

The tense form is: *is* + doing word + *-ing*

Examples: is + waiting, are + jumping, am + thinking

B. Complete the sentences with the correct doing words.

washing	climbing	combing	playing	brushing
cutting	baking	riding	running	looking

1. Sreeja is ____________________ with her dollhouse.
2. Madhu is ____________________ his hair neatly.
3. The maid is ____________________ the plates.
4. Reena is ____________________ her teeth.
5. The monkey is ____________________ a tree.
6. My brother is ____________________ a horse.
7. My father is ____________________ vegetables in the kitchen.
8. Grandma is ____________________ a cake for me.
9. The man is ____________________ for his lost ring.
10. Ramit is ____________________ after his dog.

Listening and Speaking

Learn and recite this poem.

Open a book and you will find
People and places of every kind.
Open a book and you can be
Anything you want to be.
Open a book and you can share
Wondrous words you find in there.
Open a book and I will too
You read to me and I'll read to you.

Pen it Down

Look at the picture and answer the questions. Then write the answers together as a paragraph.

- Where are the people?
- What are they looking at?
- What kind of walls do you think this place has?
- What are the creatures that can be seen?
- What do you think the people are feeling?
- Would you like to visit a place like this?

Test–1

Comprehension

A. Read this poem.

THE CLOCK

There's a neat little clock,
In the schoolroom it stands,
And it points to the time
With its two little hands.

It shows the correct time
Be it day, noon or night
Its hands are always clicking
Turning clockwise with their colours bright

And may we, like the clock,
Keep a face clean and bright,
With hands ever ready
To do what is right.

B. Answer these questions in a few lines.

1. Where does the clock stand?

____

2. What does the clock show?

____

3. Does it show the correct time?

____

4. Is the clock bright in colour?

____

5. Which body parts are mentioned in the poem?

____

6. Find rhyming words for the following words from the poem.

   a. stands __________

   b. night __________

   c. bright __________

C. Write the opposites of these words from the poem.

1. correct– __________
2. right– __________
3. clean– __________
4. stand– __________
5. clockwise– __________

D. Complete the story by choosing suitable describing words from the box.

ticking	correct	little	clearly	school	big

There is a __________ clock in the classroom. It always shows the __________ time. Children can hear the __________ sound of its hands. The clock has two __________ hands. It is kept clean so that everyone can see the time __________. The clock helps everyone reach __________ on time.

Way with Words

Rewrite the sentences using the opposites of the underlined words.

1. I could not sleep that <u>day</u> because of the strange sounds outside.

   ____

2. Rahul is a <u>fast</u> runner.

   ____

3. The <u>big</u> boy is afraid of sleeping alone at night.

   ____

4. The <u>poor</u> man was afraid of thieves.

   ____

5. There was a <u>long</u> queue in front of the ticket counter.

   ____

Grammar in Use

A. Correct the following sentences and rewrite them.

1. I is always happy to meet my cousins.

2. They was playing basketball in the garden.

3. Rahul and Vinayak am best friends.

4. Apples and bananas is very healthy.

5. He were the most hard-working student in class.

6. You is my best friend.

B. Underline the common names in this paragraph.

Tweety and Sylvester are friends. Tweety is a bird and Sylvester is a cat. They run and play under the tables and chairs all day. Last week, they broke a plate and a glass while playing. They were both punished. They were not allowed to go out of the house and run in the park. They were also not allowed to watch TV or read books. Tweety and Sylvester were very unhappy.

C. Tick the correct doing word in each sentence.

1. He like/likes sweets.
2. They sing/sings the song together.
3. I write/writes to her every month.
4. It rain/rains heavily in the month of August.
5. She sleeps/sleep like a baby.
6. The sun rise/rises in the east.
7. I can bake/bakes delicious cookies.
8. We bakes/bake delicious cakes.

Listening and Speaking

A. Listen to the following sets of words and pick the odd one out.

greet	meet	sheet	meat	bit
cake	make	bake	lake	bait
took	shock	cook	book	hook

B. Work with a partner. Imagine that you are visiting a library and want to borrow a book. Have a conversation with your partner. Your partner will be the librarian. Take turns to role-play the situation.

You can start like this:

Visitor: Good morning, Sir. I would like to borrow a book.

Librarian: Good morning! Which book would you like to borrow?

Pen it Down

Write five words, each beginning with a different vowel and make sentences with the words.

8

A Visit to the Library

Way with Words

Words Related to Books

The words in the box describe different kinds of books. Look for them in the word grid and circle them.

thriller	encyclopaedia	cookbook	poetry	drama
memoir	prose	travel	guide	fable

m	e	m	o	i	r	j	s	o	r
l	n	p	b	u	e	k	p	h	l
e	c	o	o	k	b	o	o	k	e
y	y	e	w	x	r	g	k	j	d
p	c	t	r	z	y	o	e	f	i
m	l	r	w	r	t	g	m	f	u
o	o	y	t	o	t	g	x	d	g
n	p	r	o	s	e	k	a	s	l
b	a	o	z	a	w	l	v	a	e
d	e	w	u	m	a	o	u	r	v
y	d	r	a	m	a	p	y	y	a
u	i	t	h	r	i	l	l	e	r
f	a	b	l	e	d	r	k	p	t

Grammar in Use

Possessive Pronouns

Words that can be used in place of naming words to show ownership or possession are called **possessive pronouns**.

Examples: This apple is **mine**. That blue bottle is **hers.**

A. Circle the correct possessive pronouns in these sentences.

1. The binoculars are hers/its.
2. The chocolate wafers in the fridge are all mine/them.
3. This bag is not yours/her.
4. These helmets are your/ours.
5. Are these shoes theirs/hims?

B. Fill in the blanks with the correct possessive pronouns.

1. He will finally have what is rightfully ____________. (his/her)
2. I don't have a pencil so Maya lent me ____________. (hers/yours)
3. The board game is ____________. (my/mine)
4. This cupcake is ____________ but you may have it. (him/mine)
5. That room of ____________ is so untidy. (your/yours)

Regular and Irregular Verbs

We can change most verbs from the present to the past tense by adding *-ed* or *-d* to them.

These are known as **regular verbs**.

Examples: laugh + *-ed* = **laughed**, hope + *-d* = **hoped**

Some verbs change their form completely when they are changed from the present to the past tense.

These verbs are known as **irregular verbs**.

Examples: grow → grew, think → **thought**

C. Circle the regular verbs in the paragraph. Underline the irregular verbs.

Saisha woke up from her nap and stretched. She was very tired after playing hockey for an hour. So, she took a small nap. Now she was hungry. She got up from the bed and went to the kitchen, looking for something to eat. She took an apple from the bowl of fruits kept on the kitchen table. She thought to herself, 'If only someone made me a cup of hot chocolate now!'

Listening and Speaking

Think of ten sentences on the topic 'Why I like to read'. Speak on the topic for two minutes in class.

You may talk about these points:

- Reading takes me to different places
- I meet many interesting characters when I read books
- I learn many new words

Pen it Down

Which is your favourite bedtime story? Why do you like it? Write a paragraph describing why you like it. You can also draw and colour the picture of the cover of your favourite book.

9

Hiding

Way with Words

Homophones

A. Make sentences with the following pairs of similar sounding words.

1. buy: ____________________
   by: ____________________
2. ate: ____________________
   eight: ____________________
3. break: ____________________
   brake: ____________________
4. deer: ____________________
   dear: ____________________
5. flour: ____________________
   flower: ____________________
6. mail: ____________________
   male: ____________________
7. tale: ____________________
   tail: ____________________

Rhyming Words

B. Underline the rhyming words in each sentence.

1. Dot the dog was caught sitting on the pot.
2. Can you see the wound on the knee?
3. Who will bake the cake?
4. A dog does not fail to wag its tail.

Grammar in Use

Apostrophe for Possession

You know that apostrophes can be used to show that something belongs to someone.

Examples: Is that **Tarini's** mother? **Sudeep's** cycle is new.

A. Rewrite these phrases using 's. One is done for you.

1. The bag that belongs to Samreen
   Samreen's bag
2. The motorbike that is owned by Mr Ghosh
   ____
3. The gown that belongs to my mother
   ____
4. The hut owned by the wise man
   ____
5. The parrot that belongs to Tisha
   ____

Apostrophe for Contractions

When some words are shortened, an apostrophe (') is used to replace the dropped letter(s).

Examples: **I'm** so thirsty.
He's my uncle.

Apostrophes are also used to join two words.

Example: do + not = **don't**

B. Fill in the blanks with the correct words.

1. __________ (He'll/I'm) going to the playground now.
2. __________ (It's/He'd) raining heavily today.
3. __________ (Can't/Don't) put your hands on wet paint.
4. __________ (Didn't/Mustn't) you like the book?
5. Dear Shireen, __________ (He'll/you're) my best friend.
6. __________ (He'd/I'm) meet his friend in the park every day.

7. I __________ (she'll/won't) have junk food every day.

8. Rana __________ (couldn't/don't) learn swimming this summer.

9. We wanted to attend the function, but we __________ (you're/can't).

10. __________(He'll/I'm) come home by 5 p.m.

11. We __________ (I'm/mustn't) waste food.

12. __________ (She'll/I'm) go to the park in the evening.

Using Has/Have

You have learned that verbs should agree with the subjects.

When we have a singular subject, we use *has*. We also use *has* with the pronouns *he*, *she*, and *it*.

Examples: Mary **has** a little lamb. She **has** a new bag.

When we have a plural subject, we use *have*. We use *have* with the pronouns I, *we*, *you*, and *they*.

Examples: The twins **have** a baby sister. Jaya and Simra **have** no other siblings.

C. Complete the sentences with has/have.

Raja __________ a dog and two kittens. The dog __________ a soft coat and his name is Pepper. Both the kittens __________ furry coats and are called Garlic and Ginger. Raja __________ a kennel for Pepper but the kittens __________ a basket to sleep in. Every morning Pepper __________ biscuits while the kittens __________ milk.

Listening and Speaking

Work in pairs and choose a cartoon show from the given list. Talk about it with your partner.

Tom and Jerry

Sylvester and Tweety

Adventures of Donald Duck

Scooby-Doo, Where are You?

You can begin like this:

Student 1: I was watching my favourite cartoon show on Sunday.

Student 2: Oh really? Which show?

Student 1: *Tom and Jerry* is my favourite show. I can't stop laughing when I see their naughty deeds..

Pen it Down

Have you ever been to a water theme park? Write a few sentences about your experience using the given clues.

swimming and playing in the water
enjoying water rides
paddle-boating
watching the fountain show

10 The Hen and the Apple Tree

Comprehension

Read the story carefully.

Once upon a time, a herd of elephants was living near a lake in a forest. One year, it did not rain at all, and all the lakes and rivers dried up. All the elephants were worried because they did not have enough water.

'We should look for water somewhere else,' the herd decided. They went to look for water. Soon one elephant found a lake full of water. The elephants were very happy and excited, so they all ran towards the lake. Now, a lot of rabbits were living near the new lake. The elephants were so excited that they did not notice the rabbits. A few rabbits came under their big feet by mistake. The poor rabbits were so scared!

One wise rabbit wanted to save the other rabbits. He went to the chief of the elephants and told him what had happened. He was very sad to hear about the rabbits. He said sorry and promised that the herd would be careful.

But the rabbits were so tiny that they kept getting hurt. The wise rabbit went to the chief again and told him that the Moon goddess was angry with them for hurting the rabbits. He took the elephants to the lake and showed them the wavy reflection of the moon in the lake. The wise rabbit said, 'The Moon goddess will punish you all if you do not leave this place immediately.' The elephants were scared and left the place soon. The clever rabbit saved all the other rabbits by his wit.

Read these sentences and write if they are true (T) or false (F).

1. The lakes dried up because the elephants drank up all the water. ______
2. The elephants were very happy and excited when they found the new lake. ______
3. Every day when they went to drink water, they stepped on bananas. ______
4. The chief of the elephants promised that the herd would be careful. ______
5. The rabbits were tiny so the huge elephants couldn't see them. ______
6. The wise rabbit told the elephants that the Wind god was angry. ______
7. The elephants were not scared of the reflection and laughed. ______
8. The clever rabbit saved the other rabbits. ______

Way with Words

WORDS BEGINNING WITH CR-

A. Solve the crossword with cr- words.

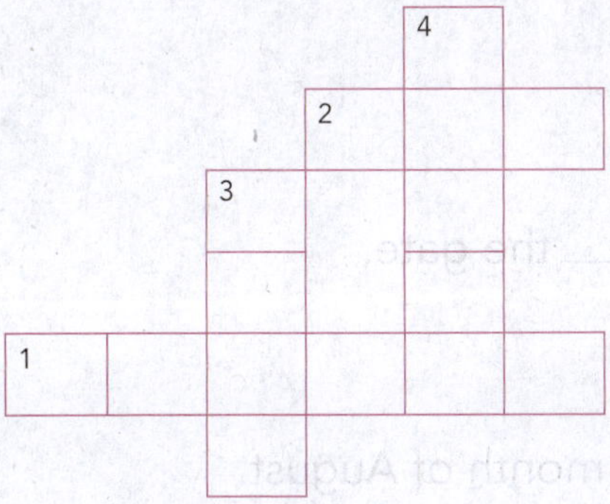

Across

1. a small bed for a child
2. shed tears

Down

3. a sea creature with claws
4. move slowly

WORDS ENDING IN -ST

B. Read the following passage and underline all the words in it that end with st.

Once upon a time, there was a dense green forest far away. One day a tired lion was returning home. On the way, he saw a cave where he thought he would stop and rest. So he went into the cave looking for some sticks. He lit a fire to stay warm.

The cave belonged to a jackal. When he returned home, he saw the lion's paw prints going into the cave. But there were none coming out. The jackal was very afraid. He grew still. He thought to himself, 'I must find a way to know if a lion is inside my cave.'

He called out, 'Hello cave, shall I come in?'

There was silence. The jackal stood still for some time. Then, again he said, 'Cave, have you forgotten to greet me? Every evening you greet me. Only then, I enter. Say hello first, or I will leave. I will go to another cave.'

The cave roared back at the jackal and asked him to enter. The jackal knew that it was the lion speaking and ran away as fast as he could.

Grammar in Use

Prepositions

Prepositions are words that tell us about the position of someone or something in relation to another.

Examples: A herd of elephants was living **near** a lake **in** a forest.

A. Fill in the blanks with prepositions from the box.

on	between	outside	at	in	inside

1. When I reached home, my dog was waiting ______ the gate.
2. Please leave your shoes ______ the door.
3. The meeting is ______ Thursday.
4. We celebrate our Independence Day ______ the month of August.
5. Keep the ball ______ the two boys.
6. It is very cold ______ the cellar at this time of the year.

B. Circle the correct options.

1. These girls will work together on/in the project.
2. The dog is running around/inside them.
3. Who is this gift to/from?
4. Mother will go to/over the bookshop tomorrow.
5. The dog is hiding outside/inside his kennel.

Adverbs

If we add *-ly* to adjectives, we can form adverbs.

Example: soft+ *-ly* = **softly**

You have learnt three types of adverbs.

Adverbs of manner tell us how something is done.

Example: The kitten purred **softly**.

Adverbs of place tell us where something is done.

Example: I found the marbles **here**.

Adverbs of time tell us when something is done.

Example: I shall see you **tomorrow**.

C. Circle the adverbs in the sentences and state their types.

1. The boy ran down the stairs quickly. ____________
2. Do not shout so loudly. ____________
3. The milkman came yesterday to deliver milk. ____________
4. The man glared at the shopkeeper angrily. ____________
5. Can you see the herd of deer there? ____________
6. Mili poured juice into the glass carefully. ____________

Listening and Speaking

Listen to the riddles and circle the correct answer.

1. car/dog/chair
2. knife/eraser/sharpener
3. ball/cold/frisbee
4. stars/moon/sun
5. your hair/your age/your hands

Pen it Down

Imagine you are the chief of the elephants. Write a letter of apology to the rabbits.
Your letter can start like this:

Dear Rabbits,

We are all so sorry to have hurt you. We did not mean to do so at all. Actually we were very excited to find the new lake and...

____

____

____

____

____

____

____

11 There Was Once a Puffin

Way with Words

Rhyming Words

Make sentences with the following sets of rhyming words.

mail – pail ______________________________

____

tree – flee ______________________________

____

swing – fling ______________________________

____

Grammar in Use

Doing Words

You know that words that show some kind of action are called **doing words.**

Examples: Charley **uses** a shovel. Father **goes** to office.

A. Complete the paragraph by using the correct forms of the verbs given in brackets.

Rahim and Rishab __________ (go) to the market on Monday. On reaching, they __________ (buy) chocolates and packets of popcorn. Rahim __________ (love) dark chocolates and Rishab __________ (like) cheese popcorn. They __________ (ask) the storekeeper where they can __________ (find) their favourite things. They both __________ (return) home smiling.

Question Words

What, when, why, who, where and *which* are called **question words**. They are used to ask questions when we want to know some information about something.

Examples: Where is Charlie's father going? **What** does Charlie use to clear the snow?

B. Complete the questions by choosing the correct word from the box. Then, write the answers to the questions. A few words might be used more than once. One is done for you.

what	why	when	where	who

1. *When* ________ *do you wake up?*
   I wake up at 7 a.m.
2. ________ is your book?
   ____
3. ________ is your sister's name?
   ____
4. ________ are you talking to?
   ____
5. ________ are you so late?
   ____
6. ________ are your exams starting?
   ____
7. ________ are you going?
   ____
8. ________ did you eat for breakfast?
   ____

Listening and Speaking

Imagine that you are a part of a class group that has to put up a programme for Independence Day. Discuss and plan what you would do. Talk about the programme with the group members.

Pen it Down

Imagine that you recently visited a bird park. Write a paragraph about your experience. You may include these points in your paragraph:

What birds did you see?

What were the colours of the birds?

Did you hear bird calls?

12 The Big Fight

Comprehension

Read this story carefully.

In the beginning, the cat and the dog were friends and lived happily with their master, Adam. They decided between themselves that the dog was to do the work outside the house and the cat inside. They put this on paper and the cat kept the agreement paper safely in the loft.

After a time, the dog was upset with the cat. One day, the dog told the cat that he was not fairly treated. He did not like to look out for thieves and protect the house, or suffer from the cold and rain outside. He was sad that he only got bones for food while the cat had all the good food and stayed near the fireplace, warm and safe.

The cat said, 'An agreement is an agreement.'

The dog replied, 'Let me see that agreement.'

The cat went quickly up the loft quickly to fetch the agreement, but it had been eaten by the mice who were living in the loft.

When the cat saw what the mice had done, she chased them away.

When she came down, the dog asked her for the agreement. As the cat had not brought it, the dog shook her until he got tired of shaking her.

Since then, when a dog meets a cat, he asks her for the agreement, and when she cannot show it to him, he chases her. And the cat, knowing that the mice are to blame, runs after the mice when she sees them.

A. Rearrange the sentences according to the order of events. Then write them as a paragraph.

☐ The cat was angry and chased the mice.

☐ The cat and dog made an agreement.

☐ Since then, a dog chases a cat and the cat chases mice.

☐ The mice had chewed up the agreement paper in the loft.

☐ The cat did all the work inside and the dog did all the work outside.

☐ In the beginning, the cat and the dog lived happily together.

☐ The cat went to the loft to fetch the agreement.

☐ Slowly the dog became unhappy staying outside, living on bones.

☐ The cat stored the agreement in the loft.

☐ The dog asked the cat to show him the agreement.

____

____

____

____

____

____

____

____

____

B. Answer the questions in brief.

1. What were the terms of the agreement?

____

2. Why did the dog feel upset?

____

____

3. What had happened to the agreement in the loft?

____

4. What did the dog do to the cat when she said she did not have the agreement?

____

____

Way With Words

Words Related to Cats and Dogs

A. Circle the pictures that are related to dogs and cats. Then match the pictures with the correct words from the box.

bone	cake	yarn	kennel	fish	bird

   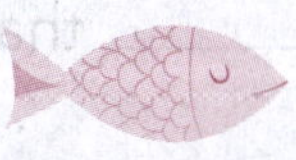 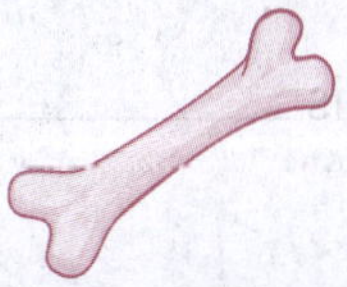 

________ ________ ________ ________ ________ ________

Word Meanings

B. Look at these words and write their meanings. You may use the dictionary.

Words	Meanings
1. beginning	
2. agreement	
3. upset	
4. fairly	
5. loft	
6. blame	

Grammar in Use

Comparative Adjectives

You know that when we compare the qualities of two naming words, we use a different form of the describing word used. We add *-er* to the describing word.

Examples: long + *-er* = **longer**   quick + *-er* = **quicker**

A. Choose the correct describing words to complete the sentences.

longer	taller	bigger	older	smaller

1. The man is ________________ than the boy.

2. The stool is ________________ than the armchair.

3. The girl is ________________ than her friend.

4. The snake is ________________ than the worm.

5. This building is ________________ than the other.

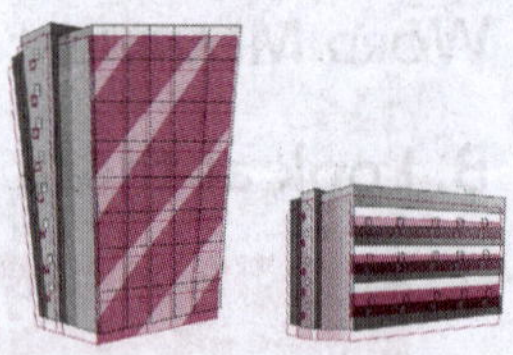

Using Myself, Yourself, Himself, Herself

When the subject and the object of an action are the same, we use these words:

I ⟶ myself　　you ⟶ yourself
he ⟶ himself　　she ⟶ herself
it ⟶ itself　　we ⟶ ourselves
they ⟶ themselves

B. Complete the sentences using myself, yourself, himself or herself.

1. Leena wrote the poem ____________.
2. I decorated the Christmas tree ____________.
3. Palak cleaned the room ____________.
4. He painted the house ____________.
5. You should do the work ____________.

Listening and Speaking

Imagine a situation where you are trying to make up with your brother or sister after a fight. What would you say to be friends again? Tell your class.

You can use the suggestions below.

- I am so sorry…
- I shouldn't have said…
- I was hurt…
- Please forgive me...

Pen it Down

Write five sentences about the Sun and the Moon by using the adjectives given in the box.

bright	dark	hot	cool
daytime	night-time	yellow	white

Sun

1. ____________________
2. ____________________
3. ____________________
4. ____________________
5. ____________________

Moon

1. ____________________
2. ____________________
3. ____________________
4. ____________________
5. ____________________

Neighbourhood and Community

13 Too Much Noise

Way with Words

Two Syllable Words

Words with two syllables are those having two vowel sounds.

Examples:

mango	pumpkin	donkey	pencil
man/go	pump/kin	don/key	pen/cil

Solve this crossword with two syllable words.

Across

3. this is used to count
5. it grows on a plant and has pretty coloured petals
6. fuel that is used to run vehicles
7. an Italian bread with toppings of vegetables and cheese

Down

1. we have ten of these on our hands
2. a sour citrus fruit
4. a person who gives medicine to sick people
6. a sea robber

Grammar in Use

ARTICLES: A, AN, AND THE

A, **an** and **the** are called **articles**. We use articles before naming words.

We use **a** and **an** for naming words that we are using for the first time, or in general. **A** is used with consonant sounds, and **an** is used before vowel sounds.

Examples: I saw **a** hen. It laid **an** egg.

The is used before naming words we have already talked about.

Example: I am eating an apple. Do you want a piece of **the** apple?

A. Complete the sentences with the articles a, an or the.

1. I have __________ apple in one hand and __________ bunch of grapes in the other.
2. __________ donkey is __________ beast of burden.
3. Sunday is __________ holiday for everybody.
4. __________ Taj Mahal is in Agra.
5. __________ egg a day and __________ glass of milk are good for health.

SIMPLE FUTURE TENSE

The **simple future tense** is used to indicate actions that are going to happen in the future. The tense form used is: **will** + doing word.

Examples: I **will start** my swimming class next summer.
The school **will reopen** in December.

B. Fill in the blanks with the correct words from the box.

will return	will finish	will shoot	will bake	will stay	will start

1. We ________ studying for our exams from next week.
2. Harshveer ________ from school in the evening today.
3. Aunt Raquel ________ some of my favourite cookies soon.
4. Do you think we ________ our homework by 6 p.m.?
5. Elina ________ with her family in Chennai when she returns from boarding school.
6. The man ________ the arrow at the apple in a few minutes.

Listening and Speaking

When we give suggestions, we should try and see that the suggestions are suitable for the person and the situation.

Example: If someone is hurt, you can suggest the following:

- Why don't you sit down and have a sip of water?
- We should call the doctor.

A. Work in pairs and give suggestions for the following situations.

1. When one has made one's mother angry
2. When one is excited about a school picnic
3. When one has forgotten to bring tiffin

B. Let us use a story ball to tell a story. As the ball is passed from hand to hand in the classroom, we can keep adding a sentence to the story.

There was an old house in the neighbourhood. No one lived there…

Now throw the ball to the next person and let him/her add a line and this is how the story will continue.

Pen it Down

You have learnt that when two people talk to one another, is it called a dialogue.

Example:

Pixy: Let us go to Raima's house to play.

Shiv: Oh no, I don't want to go there.

Pixy: Why not?

Shiv: I am afraid of her dog. He looks like he will bite me any minute.

Work in pairs and write a dialogue about a similar situation where one of you is afraid of something. You can use the following points:

- the cause behind one's fright
- steps that can be taken to stop being afraid
- how one can offer help

14 My Dad, He Wears Glasses

Way with Words

Opposite Words

Rewrite the sentences using the opposites of the underlined words.

1. Shyam's bag is very large and heavy.

____

2. These cakes and sandwiches are fresh and tasty.

____

3. My uncle is very young.

____

4. When Seema is happy, she laughs.

____

5. My neighbour is rich and lives in a big house.

____

Grammar in Use

Conjunctions: And, Or and But

Conjunctions are words that join two or more sentences, phrases, and words.

Examples: He was happy **and** content.
Grandma will eat **but** after an hour.
Do you want a piece of cake **or** a cookie?

The words **and**, **but** and **or** are conjunctions.

A. Use the words and, but and or to join these sentences. Make changes where necessary.

1. Dogs bark. Horses neigh.

   ____

2. Myra is a talented dancer. Ritu is a talented dancer.

   ____

3. It is sunny now. It might rain in the afternoon.

   ____

4. You can have a bun. You can have a cupcake.

   ____

5. Rishu can wear a yellow shirt. He can wear a brown shirt.

   ____

B. Fill in the blanks with suitable conjunctions.

1. We must reach school on time __________ the gates will be closed.
2. Soham __________ Payal are taking computer lessons.
3. Harshit is very tall __________ Nishit is rather short.
4. Milind set his alarm __________ he woke up late.
5. Bela likes to eat fish __________ chips.

Listening and Speaking

A. Listen to the instructions and colour the circles, squares and triangles.

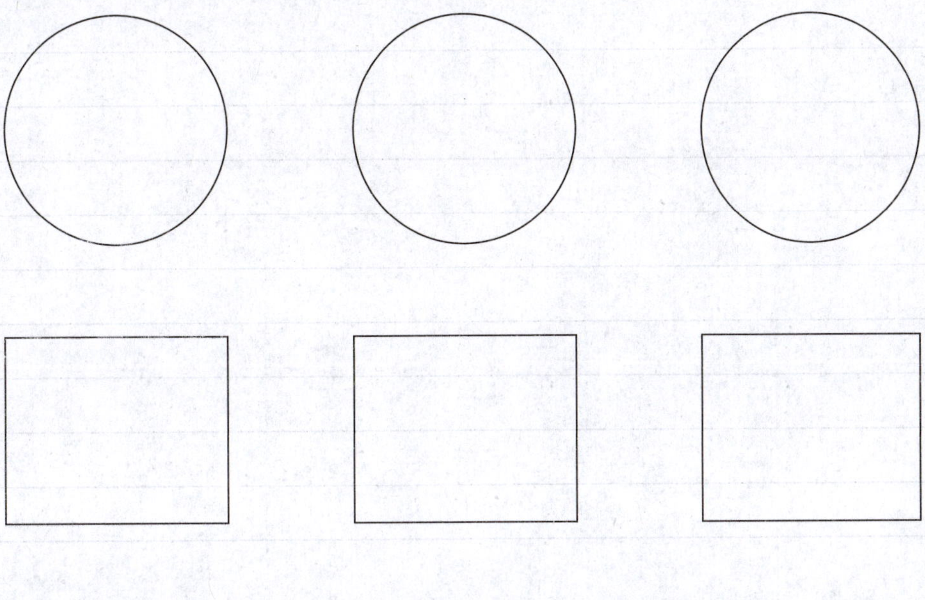

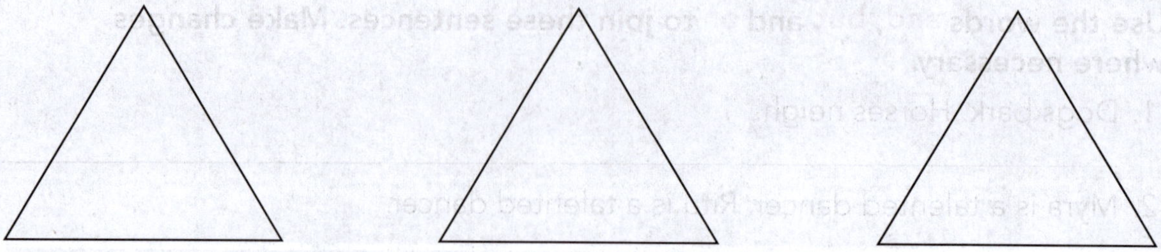

B. Losing something always makes one sad. How would you feel if you lost your favourite story book? What would happen when you found it again? Share your experience about losing and finding with your class.

Pen it Down

Read the short poem given below.

Cobbler, cobbler, mend my shoe
Give it a stitch and that will do.
Here's a nail and there's a prod,
And now my foot is well shod.

Using these pairs of rhyming words, try and write a short poem.

walk-talk   call-tall   big-wig   nap-tap   deep-sleep   fill-hill

Music

15

The Bremen Town Musicians

Comprehension

Read the story carefully and answer the questions.

Once upon a time there were three billy goats Gruff; Little billy goat, Middle billy goat and Big billy goat, who lived in a field in a green valley. They loved to eat sweet grass. Soon their field was empty because they were greedy goats, and they had eaten up all the grass. But they were still hungry. In the distance, they could see a field that was full of sweet grass. There was only one way to get to it—across a broken bridge over a stream.

But under the bridge lived a terrible troll. He was always hungry too. And there was nothing he liked better than to eat a nice juicy billy goat. Little billy goat was the first to reach the bridge. His hoof went *trip trap* on the wooden bridge. Suddenly there was a huge roar from the troll.

'Who is that on my bridge?'

Little billy goat Gruff managed to squeak, 'I am going to look for some grass to eat.'

'Oh no, you are not! I am going to eat you!' roared the troll.

'Please do not eat me,' said scared Little billy goat Gruff. 'I am just Little billy goat Gruff. Wait for my brother. He is bigger than me.'

So, the greedy troll decided to wait and let Little billy goat Gruff cross the bridge.

Next, Middle billy goat Gruff began to cross the bridge. *Trip, trap* went his hooves.

Again, the troll roared, 'Who is that on MY bridge?'

Middle billy goat Gruff said in his softest voice, 'I am following my brother, Little billy goat Gruff, so I can eat the grass.'

'I am going to eat you!' said the troll.

'But I am not big enough. Wait until my big brother comes along.'

'Alright,' said the troll.

Middle billy goat Gruff ran over the bridge and began to eat the grass with Little billy goat Gruff.

Big billy goat Gruff was next. Bravely, he put his hooves onto the bridge. Suddenly the troll jumped out from under the bridge.

'Who is that trip trapping over MY bridge?' he boomed.

'It is me, Big billy goat Gruff. Who do you think you are?' asked Big billy goat Gruff, loudly.

'I am the troll, and I am going to eat you.'

'Oh no, you will not!'

Then the troll rushed at Big billy goat Gruff. Big billy goat Gruff bent his head and threw the troll into the stream below.

The troll disappeared under the water and was gone.

From then on, anyone could cross the bridge and enjoy the green grass.

A. Read the lines from the story and answer the questions.

'Please do not eat me,'

a. Who said these words and to whom?

____

b. What had the speaker done for it to be eaten by the listener?

____

____

c. Did the person spoken to listen to these words? Why/why not?

____

____

B. Complete the following sentences.

1. The billy goats' field was bare because _______________
2. Under the bridge lived _______________
3. Middle billy goat Gruff was crossing the bridge when _______________
4. Big billy goat bent his head and _______________
5. After that, anyone _______________

C. Answer the following questions.

1. What could the three billy goats see in the distance?

____

2. What did the troll like to eat?

____

3. How did Middle billy goat save himself?

4. What did Big billy goat tell the troll?

5. What happened to the troll?

Way with Words

Names of Professions

A. Match the pictures in Column B with the professions in Column A.

Column A	Column B
1. chef	a. 
2. firefighter	b. 
3. nurse	c. 
4. pilot	d. 

Anagrams

B. Rearrange the letters of each anagram to match the meaning.

1. beats: ____________________
   Meaning: an animal or living creature
2. strait: ____________________
   Meaning: a person who paints pictures for a living
3. arches: ____________________
   Meaning: to look for something
4. rested: ____________________
   Meaning: an area full of sand and dunes
5. heart: ____________________
   Meaning: the planet on which we all live

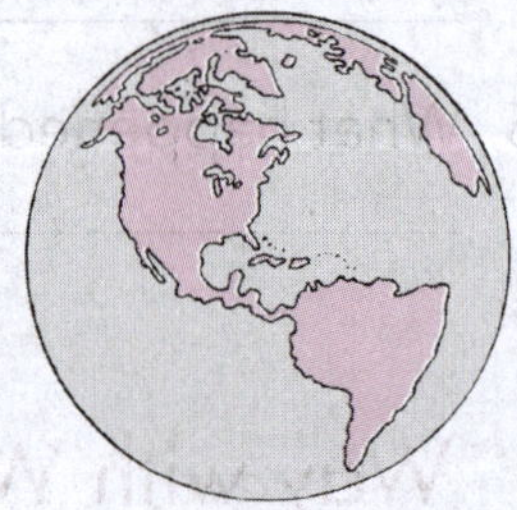

Grammar in Use

Forming Negative Sentences

We use the words 'not' or 'no' to say something negative.

Examples: This is **not** my cycle. **No** shop is open now.

A. Change the sentences into the negative form by adding the word not.

1. I am studying for the exam.

   ____

2. He was interested in reading the book.

   ____

3. She was waiting for her mother's permission.

   ____

4. My friends are worried about my safety.

   ____

5. I have finished my dinner.

   ____

Using Much or Many

When we talk about uncountable nouns, we use **much**. When we talk about countable nouns, we use **many**.

Examples: My phone does not have **much** power.
Mother gave me **many** hugs.

Similarly, we use **how much** to ask questions about uncountable nouns, and **how many** to ask questions about countable nouns.

Examples: **How much** time did you take to get here?
How many monkeys can you see?

B. Complete the sentences with much or many.

1. How ________________ milk do you want?
2. How ________________ strawberries are there in the basket?
3. How ________________ children attended the birthday party?
4. How ________________ questions do you have for homework?
5. How ________________ does this dress cost?

Listening and Speaking

A. Listen to the descriptions and name the animals correctly.

1. ________________ 2. ________________

3. ________________ 4. ________________

5. ________________

B. Work in groups of four. Act out a scene from the play, *The Bremen Town Musicians*. You can choose the part where the four musicians are feeling hungry after seeing the food and continue to the part where they make a noise and frighten the robbers.

Pen it Down

Look at these jumbled clues telling a story. Arrange the clues in the right order and then write the story.

The door slammed—mother was wide awake—the dog was barking—a loud scream—the thief was stealing money—the police came—mother was relieved—thief taken to jail.

Test–2

Comprehension

A. Read the following passage and answer the questions.

The Sandy Cat

The sandy cat sat by the kitchen fire. Yesterday, she had no food. This morning, everyone forgot to give her food. All she wanted was a little grey mouse, a saucerful of milk and a few fish or chicken bones. But there was no mouse, milk or fish. The serving maid was busy washing clothes and hanging them out to dry. The children were still on their way to school. The father and mother had both gone to work and grandmother sat making a patchwork quilt. No one thought of the sandy cat, who was sitting by the fire, alone and hungry.

At last the clothes were washed and the children came back from school. The serving maid put on a white apron and took the cat in her arms. She said, 'Kitty, shall we go into the garden?' So they went and walked in the garden. They stopped before a rose bush. The maid held up the cat to smell the roses. The sandy cat got annoyed, jumped from her arms and ran away. She was hungry and angry too!

1. Where was the sandy cat sitting?

____

2. Why was the sandy cat upset?

____

3. What was the serving maid doing?

____

4. Do you think the sandy cat got her dinner in the end?

____

B. Complete the sentences with words from the passage.

1. Sandy cat wanted to eat ____________, ____________ and ____________.
2. The ____________ was washing the ____________.
3. The ____________ were on their way to ____________.

Way with Words

A. Rearrange the letters of these words to form anagrams.

1. takes ____________
2. lore ____________
3. tale ____________
4. grate ____________
5. care ____________
6. tool ____________

B. Match the words with their meanings.

Words	Meanings
1. happy	a. close
2. start	b. ill
3. big	c. save
4. little	d. wealthy
5. shut	e. begin
6. quick	f. loud
7. keep	g. glad
8. sick	h. large
9. noisy	i. fast
10. rich	j. small

Grammar in Use

A. Circle the adverbs and underline the doing words they describe.

1. Tigers can run very quickly.
2. The boy cried sadly when he lost his colouring book.
3. The singer sang joyfully.

4. Rohan smiled sweetly for the camera.
5. They ran to the bus stop hurriedly.

B. Read the sentences and write suitable questions for them.

1. I live in Bangalore.

____

____

2. My brother's name is Arihant.

____

____

3. Yes, it is very hot today.

____

4. No, I am not playing tennis today.

____

5. These are my books.

____

6. Her favourite colour is green.

____

7. There are 40 students in the class.

____

8. I go for dance practice every Thursday.

____

Listening and Speaking

A. If you get a fairy's magical power, what are the two things you would like to do? Tell the class.

Pen it Down

Have you ever forgotten anything important, which got you in trouble? Write a short paragraph describing the incident.